Let's go and visit
Chester the Mouse,
As he searches for letters
All round the house.
He wants to discover
His own ABC
And may need some help
From you and from me.
Close on his heels
There's a curious cat,
But Chester's too busy
To think about that.
He gathers up letters
To make his own store,
But if you look carefully
You'll often see more.

This book was first published in 1989 by
Advanced Marketing Services, Inc.
San Diego, CA 92117

World Copyright, Text & Illustrations © Princess House, 1989

All rights reserved. No part of this publication
may be reproduced, stored in a retrieval system,
or transmitted, in any form or by any means, electronic,
mechanical, photocopying, recording or otherwise,
without the prior permission of the copyright holder.

Text written by Jacqueline Fortey and Antony Atha

ISBN 0-934429-49-9

Printed and bound Hungary

CHESTER THE MOUSE
ABC ALPHABET BOOK

ILLUSTRATED BY JANE HARVEY

BUTTERSCOTCH BOOKS

Aa

With his nose in the air,
Chester's off on his way.
In this alphabet story
He's found letter A!

Abacus   Ace   Acorn   Acrobat   Alarm clock

Alligator   Anchor   Ape   Apple

Bb

Yes, Chester – you've got it!
A bright, bouncy B.
Boat, beads, box and basket,
What else can you see?

Ball   Banana   Basket   Beads   Bear   Bee   Bib   Birds   Blanket   Boat   Box   Bubbles   Butterfly

Candles   Cards   Castle   Cat   Caterpillar   Cherries

Cake, candles and cherries,
A large cup of tea,
A chocolate chip cookie,
That's Chester's own   !

Dd

Dalmatian dog   Dice   Dog tag

D's for dalmatian,
And doll's house and dice.
There's a tag on his collar
That looks rather nice.

Doll's house   Dots   Duck   Dungarees

Ee

E stands for elephant,
Chester take care!
Max the Cat's watching
On top of the chair.

Eagle   Ears   Egg

Elephant chair   Elephant egg cup   Envelope   Eyes

Ff

Chester is startled;
Frog's started to hop.
If our mouse takes the key,
That frog will soon stop.

'F'-shaped key   Feather   Fifty   Fish   Flag   Floor

Flowers   Forget-me-nots   Foot   Fort   Fox   Frog   Funny face

Gg

Game   Gift   Giraffe   Girl   Glasses   Glove

FISHING GAME

GLUE

G

The golden G glistens
But Chester can't swim.
Perhaps that nice goldfish
Will give it to him.

Glue   Goldfish   Goose   Grapes   Gravel

stands for handkerchief,
Hand cream and house,
And also for hiding . . .
Now where is that mouse?

Hand cream   Handkerchief   Hairbrush   Hair comb

HOME
SWEET
HOME

Hat   Hatpin   Heart   Hen   House

I i

Chester looks worried.
Can you see why?
He has covered the wall
With a big purple I.

Ink   Ink blot   Ink bottle   Inky footprints   Ink pen

Jj

Jack and the juggler
Ask Chester to play,
But all that he wants
Is the red letter J.

Jack-in-the-box   Jaguar   Japanese doll

Jello mold   Jewel   Jigsaw   Jug   Juggler

K k

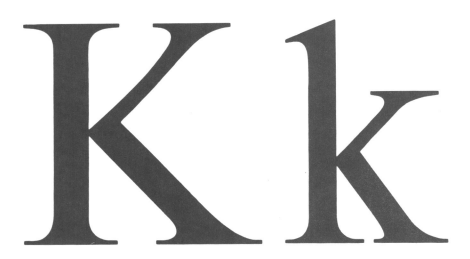

K is for knitting,
Kaleidoscope, kite,
And a kind kangaroo
Who is holding on tight
To a king in his pouch:
Chester thinks it's just right.

Kaleidoscope   Kangaroo   Kettle   Key
Kite   King   Knife   Knitting

L1

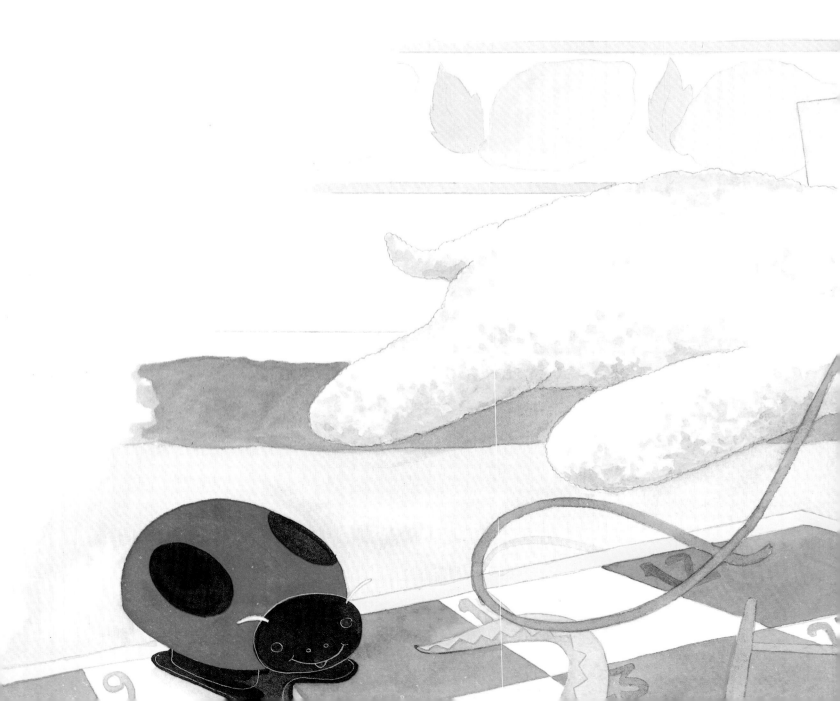

Lamb, ladybird, lemon,
Or lollipop sweet?
Chester's chosen the L
Children like as a treat.

Ladder
Ladle   Ladybird   Lamb
Legs   Lemon   Letter   Lime
Lion   Lollipop   Loop

Mm

M is for matches,
And merry-go-round,
And for the magician
That Chester has found.

Magician
Magnifying glass

Map
Mask

Matches
Max

Maze
Mermaid

Merry-go-round
Monkey

Moons
Moustache

Musical notes

Nn

N is in notebook,
Noah's Ark, nose and nest,
But Chester shows clearly
The one he likes best.

Nail   Neck   Nest   Net
Noah's ark   Noses   Notebook   Notes

Notes

Oo

This orange is juicy
And hard to resist.
What other O words
Can we add to our list?

Oak leaf   Oats   Octagon   Octopus

Old English Sheepdog   Orange   Owl   Ox

P p

Penguin or panda,
Pen, paintbrush or pie –
There's plenty to choose from.
Which one will he spy?

Padlock   Paint brushes   Panda   Parrot   Patch   Pen   Pencil

Penguin   Pie   Pineapple   Pine tree   Plane   Primrose   Purse

Qq

Quilt, queen or quacker?
Chester's so proud,
As the duck rolls along,
Quack-quack-quacking aloud.

Quacking duck   Quarter to twelve   Queen   Quill   Quilt

R r

Rattle or robin,
Rabbit or ring,
Quick, Chester, hurry,
A ribbon's the thing!

Rabbit   Rag doll   Rattle   Ribbons   Robin   Rocking horse   Rosebud   Ruby ring   Rug

Shampoo and shellfish,
Shrimp, sponge and spade,
And the bubbly pink soap,
With which Chester has played.

Scrub brush   Seal   Shampoo   Shells   Shrimp

Soap   Sponge   Starfish   Stripes   Suds   Sun

Tt

Train, tail or toucan,
Teddy's T is the best;
If Chester pulls hard
It will come off his chest.

Tail   Tangle   Teapot   Teddy   Ten past ten   Thread   Three   Time

Tomato   Top   Toucan   Train   Tree   Triangle   Trumpet   T-shirt

Umbrella   Unicycle   Uniform   Up

Chester is rushing,
He's on his way down
To the broken umbrella
Just next to that clown.

Vv

With cutting and pasting,
With ribbons and glue,
Chester's Valentine message
Reads "Max, I love you".

Valentine card   Violets

Ww

W for windmill,
Watch, wigwam and wink.
Chester sits on the wheel
As he pauses to think.

Well   West   Whale   Wheel   Whistle   Wigwam

Windmill   Wink   Witch   Wood   Wool

Xx

Max puts out a paw.
Did he win the game?
He likes letter X
At the end of his name.

X pieces

Yy

That's a very big yawn,
Max is ready for bed,
Unaware of the Y
Dangling over his head.

YEAR

Zz

Now Zachary's painting
Is pinned to the wall,
With giraffe, zoo and zebra,
Goodbye now, that's all!

Zebra   Zoo   Zoo keeper

ZOO

at the zoo

Zachary.

My Very own ALPHABET

... at last

by Chester

A
Abacus
Ace
Acorn
Acrobat
Alarm clock
Alligator
Anchor
Ape
Apple

B
Ball
Banana
Basket
Beads
Bear
Bee
Bib
Birds
Blanket
Boat
Box
Bubbles
Butterfly

C
Candles
Cards
Castle
Cat
Caterpillar
Cherries
Chester
Chocolate cake
Cookies
Crack
Crackers
Crumbs
Cup

D
Dalmatian dog
Dice
Dog tag
Doll's house
Dots
Duck
Dungarees

E
Eagle
Ears
Egg
Elephant chair
Elephant egg cup
Envelope
Eyes

F
'F'-shaped key
Feather
Fifty
Fish
Flag
Floor
Flowers
Forget-me-nots
Foot
Fort
Fox
Frog
Funny face

G
Game
Gift
Giraffe
Girl
Glasses
Glove
Glue
Goldfish
Goose
Grapes
Gravel

H
Hand cream
Handkerchief
Hairbrush
Hair comb
Hat
Hatpin
Heart
Hen
Hiding
House

I
Ink
Ink blot
Ink bottle
Inky footprints
Ink pen

J
Jack-in-the-box
Jaguar
Japanese doll
Jello mold
Jewel
Jigsaw
Jug
Juggler

K
Kaleidoscope
Kangaroo
Kettle
Key
Kite
King
Knife
Knitting

L
Ladder
Ladle
Ladybird
Lamb
Legs
Lemon
Letter
Lime

Lion
Lollipop
Loop

M Magician
Magnifying glass
Map
Mask
Matches
Max
Maze
Mermaid
Merry-go-round
Monkey
Moons
Moustache
Musical notes

N Nail
Neck
Nest
Net
Noah's ark
Noses
Notebook
Notes

O Oak leaf
Oats
Octagon
Octopus
Old English Sheepdog
Orange
Owl
Ox

P Padlock
Paint brushes
Panda
Parrot
Patch
Pen
Pencil

Penguin
Pie
Pineapple
Pine tree
Plane
Primrose
Purse

Q Quacking duck
Quarter to twelve
Queen
Quill
Quilt

R Rabbit
Rag doll
Rattle
Ribbons
Robin
Rocking horse
Rosebud
Ruby ring
Rug

Scrub brush
Seal
Shampoo
Shells
Shrimp
Soap
Sponge
Starfish
Stripes
Suds
Sun

T Tail
Tangle
Teapot
Teddy
Ten past ten
Thread

Three
Time
Tomato
Top
Toucan
Train
Triangle
Trumpet
T-shirt

U Umbrella
Unicycle
Uniform
Up

V Valentine card
Violets

W Watch
Well
West
Whale
Wheel
Whistle
Wigwam
Windmill
Wink
Witch
Wood
Wool

X X pieces

Y Yacht
Yawn
Year
Yoyo

Z Zebra
Zoo
Zoo keeper

Did you know which letters
Chester would choose,
Rushing around
With no time to lose,
With Max, his cat friend,
Not far behind
Wondering how many words
He could find?
All of the objects
He found in the house
Now belong to
This tired little mouse,
Who dreamed of the
Alphabet letters he took,
As he yawned and curled up
At the end of your book.